Z-DAY

SURVIVING THE ZOMBIE APOCALYPSE

S. David Staggs

Dedicated to my mother and daughter and group...

And to all those preparing to survive the dead...

SECTION ONE

ZOMBIES

When it comes to surviving a zombie apocalypse, or any apocalypse, it's most important to know your enemy. So let's go over this terrifying threat and the varied forms they could come in. We're going to break these zombies up into two types:

1. **The Undead Type**

2. **The Living Type**

The undead type would be what most would think of when hearing the word "zombie." They are the living dead, a reanimated corpse, mindless, and aggressive, with basic primitive instincts. Most would consider them rigid and slow moving, but very dangerous – especially in large groups, most commonly referred to as "hordes".

The dangers from an undead zombie would be many. Disease they carry from rotting tissue, infection from bites or scratches, and unrelenting pressure when they grab due to dead nerves. The worst part is they feel no pain and have no sense of fear – they just keep coming with no sense of self preservation. That alone makes them an enemy unlike any other threat you would encounter.

However, the living zombie would have some of the same traits, but being alive, they could run. So imagine if you will now, something fearless and aggressive that can run. The stakes just got higher for survival. But there *is* some balance with this! Where the undead zombie, in theory, can only be stopped by severe head trauma, a living zombie could be stopped by a wider range of means.

These are the basic definitions of zombies that this book will go by, but other aspects, like mutation and causes, will be discussed in later sections! There is much to consider in an apocalypse; what to eat, where to hide, who to trust, where to go. All these questions and more will be answered in the pages that follow!

Are you prepared?

SECTION TWO

OTHER THREATS

A lot of people think of only the zombie threat when they ponder a zombie apocalypse. They couldn't be more wrong! Zombies will be the main threat, out numbering humans, but not the only threat. One of the biggest threats will be other people. You now have no government, no police, and no system. Everything about normal society has collapsed, which means criminals and bandits will cause many problems for decent people trying to survive.

Although the right thing to do is help others in need, you won't be able to lower your guard around people you don't know anymore. Clever bandits will act like decent people, set traps, act hurt, simply to ambush you and steal your supplies...or worse! This will be something you have to trust your instincts on. All you can hope for is that you help the right ones, and avoid those looking to do harm.

Another threat that is not always considered is insects. We know there are viruses that cannot be transmitted by a mosquito. We also know there are some that can be, like West Nile. What happens if the zombie virus (assuming it's a virus) can be transmitted through mosquito bites? It'll spread even faster! We could assume that mosquitos would be deterred away from the undead type, due to their horrible smell and decaying tissue...but the living type? That's a different story altogether!

Now zombies and human dangers aside, you have to worry about water supply and food supply. Malnutrition and dehydration are also going to be a threat. In the event of a zombie apocalypse the best thing you can do is fill containers and the bath tub full of water while you can. Then gather all your non-perishables and secure your home or whatever dwelling you're in at the time. It's even more advisable to stock up on bottled water and things like canned goods, rice and dry beans. We'll cover the stock list later on.

Let's not forget the elements. The summer heat is survivable in shelter, but eventually winter will set in. Even in a shelter, you won't last long in freezing temperatures. Eventually the power will fail, and it won't be coming back on. Some may have gas generators, and that's good in many disasters, but the noise is like ringing the dinner bell for any zombies in the area. Not to mention alerting bandits. So find some warm blankets, and again, it's advisable to buy a bulk pack of thermal blankets. Once things settle, it may be the best interest of your group to discuss taking the risk of hitting the road to a warmer climate.

Last, but certainly not least, is the threat of illness and injury. If you have a doctor in your group, consider yourself lucky, since hospitals will be a thing of the past. Although sometimes taking risks will be inevitable, carefully weigh out all options beforehand. A broken bone could be the difference between life and death.

SECTION THREE

SAFE HOUSES

Next to supplies and weapons, your greatest concern will be shelter and fortification. This is something you will have to carefully consider with your family and group. It will be one of the most important choices you'll face. Some people already have this all planned out, but ninety-nine percent do not. Let's go over what to consider and look for in a safe house for you and your loved ones.

There are many factors you are going to have to weigh in on depending on where you live; city, country, suburbs, etc. For example, if you live in the country, and have plans, you could act on them even in the height of the chaos. On the other end of the spectrum, this would be a bad idea in a highly populated city. If you reside in a city, your safest bet is to fortify your doors and windows. Just the door if you're in a high rise apartment. From there, sit tight. Ration the food and supplies you have as long as possible. Once the initial chaos has calmed down after a few weeks then would be the time to pack up and head out to find a better location.

Some will want to stay in their homes, which is a natural response. Homes are harder to fortify, however. If you're living in a one story house, you would have to board up all the windows and doors but still have an escape route planned. And even so, a large enough horde of zombies, who have discovered you, could eventually get through your boarded windows.

In a second story home, you could fortify the entire bottom floor, and destroy the staircase. Replace the staircase with a ladder and even if your bottom floor is compromised, you have the upstairs. But now you're trapped there. Just an example of how a good plan can go to hell rather quickly. Definitely something to think about!

Another thing to think about when considering using your home is the threat of fire. It wouldn't take much for bandits to try and burn you out. Also try not to set any zombies on fire; they will still try to breach your home and now have the ability to set it ablaze. Food for thought! Now, if you have a brick home that will be a lesser concern.

If your home is surrounded by a chain link security fence and completely gated in, that is a plus for staying home and fortifying what you have. Depending on how secure it is, it will keep the dead out for a while or altogether (depending on zombie horde sizes). This will also give you more time to safely fortify your home inside and out. However, a group of bandits could also just drive through the fence in an assault on your safe house.

Let's go over the things to look for in a safe house:

- Limited to no windows

- More than one exit

- Steel or thick wooden doors

- Isolated as much as possible

- Close enough to towns for raiding supplies

- Easily defendable

- Roof access

You won't likely find a place with all of these, but those are key things to look at. The more the better! You don't want to be anywhere that is full of glass doors and windows. You're just asking for trouble if you choose such a location. If it has only one glass door that you could solidly block off, go for it. If not, I advise to keep searching for a long term safe house.

Here are some good ideas for a safe house:

- JAIL/PRISON – If not in the heart of a city or larger town, a jail or Juvenile Detention Center would be an amazing safe house. Brick, fenced in and easily defendable.

- FARM – Provided it is very isolated and you've taken the time to really fortify it, this could be a longer term safe house; but I wouldn't hope for it to last forever.

- BARS – Most bars or pubs have limited windows and steel or wooden doors. Although this might not be the best long term shelter, it could buy you some time to rest awhile.

- STORAGE UNITS – Most wouldn't even think to consider this, but they are well suited. Most are fenced in, have multiple larger buildings with no windows and are easily defendable.

- WAREHOUSE/FACTORY – These are another good consideration. A lot of them have few windows, some are fenced in, and many are isolated or on the outside limits of towns.

Think about where you live and come up with multiple buildings like these. Remember, you might have a plan...but always have a plan B and C. After all, it is very possible you can go to your first location and discover someone else already made it their own. Plan ahead and accordingly! Sometimes buildings get demolished or destroyed. Keep track of your planned locations and have a meeting with your family and group every so often to keep things fresh in mind.

Now that we have discussed places to go, we'll go over places to avoid:

- <u>THE CITY</u> – Any city is a bad idea unless you have no other choice for supplies. The streets will be littered with the dead and other threats.

- <u>RETAIL STORE</u> – This is only worth carefully raiding; not for shelter. They are nothing but large windows, glass doors, and far too large to safely defend.

- <u>HOSPITAL</u> – The only good reason to go to a hospital would be for gathering medical supplies, and only if you had no other options. A hospital would likely have many zombies wandering the halls from everyone that ended up trapped there when the apocalypse started. The building is too large to take such risks. If you need medical supplies, go to pharmacies, doctors' offices, and smaller med centers.

- <u>SCHOOLS</u> – To some this may sound like a good idea, but don't forget that many schools are large and mostly consist of glass doors and many windows. In the end, this could easily become a death trap.

- <u>APARTMENT BUILDINGS</u> – Again, far too large and more than likely crawling with the infected.

- <u>GOVERNMENT SAFE HOUSES</u> – At the height of the chaos, you'll be informed about safe havens being put together for survivors and refugees. If you choose to risk that route, I wish you the best and hope it works out. That many people trying to gain access to one place could easily turn into a disaster. Especially if a massive horde shows up and the safe house falls. You're better off hitting the road with your group.

Scout carefully, trust your instincts and just use common sense. Remember: Panic and fear can cause you or your groups' demise. Stay collected and clear headed.

SECTION FOUR

WEAPONS

In this section we will go over what weapons/tools you should consider having in your supply and which ones you could stand to leave behind. We'll start with weapons that you should try and obtain, followed by ones to avoid. Some are obvious choices, others not so much!

WEAPONS TO OBTAIN

CROWBAR – The crowbar should be a must have in your supplies. Not only is this tool great for raids to open locked doors, but it's a wonderful weapon! It is not too heavy, can cause great damage to a zombie's skull, and is very durable!

MACHETE – Eventually your group may find itself in wooded areas and you'll need to cut through some foliage. Not only that, this thing will effectively slice into a zombie's skull. Make sure you keep it sharp though, as with any bladed weapons.

COMBAT KNIFE – One of these should be on you at all times when away from your safe house. You never know when you could end up in close quartered combat while out on a raid. If threatened by a hostile bandit, this could save your life, as well as with a zombie. Just stab the blade through the eye socket or base of the skull. Remember to find a good quality fixed blade knife.

SLINGSHOT – This is **NOT** for defense, but should be added to your supply. You want to conserve ammunition so use this for quiet, small game hunting around the safe house.

HIGH POWERED AIR RIFLE – You probably never thought to put this on your list, but I recommend it! You might be surprised to learn that some of these can put down a coyote. If you have a rifle that is over 1,000 FPS, this can come in handy! At close range, this could possibly penetrate the skull of a lone zombie wandering in your area. At the very least, again, this is great for small game hunting around your safe house. Don't rely on this for zombie defense. You'll do good to maybe take out one at close range, if you hit the right spot.

HAMMER – You may need this to help fortify whatever you have chosen as a safe house. If you're boarding up a window and a zombie pops through a good penetrating strike to the skull will drop it. But this is very close combat and not recommended as a zombie defense side arm.

AXE – An axe will serve you well in such an event. You may need to cut through a door or wall, and an axe will stop a zombie with one well-placed strike. Just make sure you are grounded well, don't risk getting killed by the mistake of losing balance with a heavy weapon. Also, if your safe house is near a wooded area, you'll need this to get fire wood.

HATCHET – What's an axe without its little counterpart? This will also assist with fire wood and other chores, and if need be, will protect you dearly from a zombie that catches you off guard.

SHOTGUN – This should be another must have. It has massive stopping power against a group of zombies or bandits. This is a weapon that causes extreme damage, and can do that damage to more than one target at a time. This could save your life. There's only one major issue, and this isn't just for shotguns, it is for any firearm you have: Noise. Zombies will likely be drawn to noise and wander toward the source. This could put you in a pinch, so try and only use firearms when there is no other option. Don't waste a shell or bullet on one zombie, only to attract a huge horde that may be somewhere close by.

RIFLE – This will have two basic functions for a zombie pandemic. If a raid goes bad, and a horde surrounds fellow group members, you could do well to have a rifle. Whoever is the best shot, should be place somewhere away from the raid, and be able to cover the rest of the group. This also applies if hostile bandits show up.

PISTOL – These make for a good side arm when raiding in smaller areas, like homes or trailers. The only flaw here is the possibility of the gun jamming. This would be the opportune time to grab that combat knife we discussed earlier!

REVOLVER – The same concept applies here as with the pistol. Holds less rounds, but you don't have to worry about the jamming issue.

BOW AND ARROW – Not everyone is a good archer, but surely someone in your group will be at least decent. This weapon comes in different forms: long bow, recurve bow, and compound bow. A well placed arrow will quietly drop a zombie, as well as game for food. However, I would not advise this weapon in a horde situation, unless you're out of their reach and have a decent amount of arrows.

CROSSBOW – Another great and efficient silent weapon. With the crossbow, unlike other bows, you can take your time aiming. Aside from that, all the same applies compared to bows.

KATANA – Swords might not be the most well suited weapons for zombies, but if you want one, choose the Katana. It's more light weight but highly effective. You could cut off zombie heads with little effort, or also pierce the skull with the end of the blade. But, if you're going to acquire a katana, make absolutely sure it is a real one and not a show piece. A show piece will eventually just break and put you at high risk.

WEAPONS TO AVOID

SLEDGE HAMMER – The main problem here is the tools weight. This could easily throw you off balance and get you killed pretty fast. Also, no one wants to constantly carry around such a heavy weapon. Lastly, although one shot to the head would drop any zombie, you better time the strike just right and hope you don't miss. This tool is better off tossed aside.

TWO-HANDED SWORD – Let's just get this one out of the way quickly. The same issues apply here that would a sledge hammer. A giant sword is not practical in any way for this kind of situation.

CHAINSAW – This would probably be the worst weapon idea you could ever consider for the living dead. Don't forget that zombies are the result of an infection of some sort! The last thing you want is to be covered with a zombie's blood, risking infection due to contact with the eyes or any open wounds. Even if this wasn't an issue, the noise factor alone should rule this out. Just forget all power tools!

THROWING KNIVES – This here is another prime example of something to leave on the shelf. Don't take up valuable supply room with something like throwing knives. The likelihood of you actually hitting a zombie is very low. Unless, of course, you were already a knife throwing professional pre-apocalypse, then have at it.

SHOVEL – This is a useful tool and it's fine to have one of these in the group, but not as a weapon. Too much use in combat and a shovel will end up breaking over a zombie's head, and leave you with a piece of wood. Leave it in the tool shed.

BOOMERANG – Sometimes people are surprised to see certain warning labels on products, and wonder who would do that. Those warnings are there because sure enough, someone tried. For that reason I have added the Boomerang. Someone would probably actually try this out, but it's not a wise idea. At most it will hit a zombie, irritate it, and make it aware of you. At worst, it will miss, fly back, and possibly knock you out...all the while still making the zombie aware of you. Now you're the zombies' next meal, congratulations! Unless you're an Australian Aborigine dealing with zombies, leave the Boomerang alone. They know how to use it. You likely do not.

FLAMETHROWER – This goes back to what we discussed before. Flaming zombies are very bad. Let's say you are holed up in some old farm house. The last thing you need is a/are burning zombie/zombies still trying to get into your shelter. Now your shelter is on fire as well. If you come upon a flamethrower, just leave it alone. Nothing good will come of it and the risks are just too high. And let's face it; there are much easier ways to get a camp fire started on those cooler nights.

MACHINE GUNS – When it comes to the undead variety of zombies only a head shot, in theory, will drop them permanently. This is why shotguns, rifles, and handguns suffice. With a machine gun you're simply going to waste a lot of ammunition. If you start shooting at a horde, you'll achieve some head shots, but you'll surely miss plenty too. On the flip side, if you're dealing with living zombies, this will be more acceptable to use. If you happen upon a machine gun, by all means, take it! It may not be worth much against undead zombies...but for bandits it would be a great asset.

SPEAR – Here we have a weapon that is fine for hunting and fishing if need be, but NOT for ghoul defense. If you throw a spear at a zombie, I hope you're a good shot. If you miss, your weapon is lost. Also, if there are more than one and you hit, your weapon is still lost with more hostile corpses coming at you. Discard the spear altogether as a weapon.

SYTHE – The sythe is an old tool for mowing grass and reaping crops, and believe it or not, is still used in certain parts of Asia and Europe today. One issue is this tool has some weight and it's large to carry around. That alone rules it as more trouble than it's worth. This would easily decapitate a zombie or pierce a skull, but in a horde situation, you're on the losing side.

PICKAXE – Here's another hefty one that you really don't want to haul around. With a long thin blade on one end, and a long pick on the other, this naturally would do serious damage. But the same rule applies here as applied to the sledgehammer: You'll need to time your shot and hope you hit the target. My best advice is leaving it in the garage.

When it comes to choosing a weapon, just think common sense for the situation. Apply the rules of weight and effect, accuracy, noise factor, and how close you have to get for a certain encounter. When the Zombie Apocalypse begins, the main thing to remember is common sense and keeping a cool head. Stay as calm as possible to collect thoughts and gather things you need to fight through this. Panic will be your worst enemy, over the ghouls and bandits.

SECTION FIVE

FOOD SUPPLY

Your supply and choices of food are one of the most important for your group to survive. It's nothing to take likely by any means...without energy and hydration you'll be in no shape to defend against zombie hordes or bandits that want your supplies. We're going to carefully go over important items that you should stock up on and have ready to move on a moment's notice. If you're not stocked up when disaster occurs, then these items are what you will want to scavenge for.

<u>WATER</u> – Water is the most valuable of supplies. Without water, you won't last longer than one week. Keep a decent stock pile of this, and if you're really in luck, your safe house will be near a water supply. Just make sure you boil any water you find. Also, you don't really need to pay attention to the expiration date on bottled water. The state of New Jersey requires by law all items to have an expiration date. So to avoid issues in shipping, all water companies throw a best by date on it. Over time residual plastic may creep into the water, but we're talking about a low percent over many, many years. At most, the water will have an off taste. Besides, slightly off taste water will be the least of your worries.

<u>BEANS</u> – Bags of dried beans pretty much last forever. Try to stock or locate a good supply of these.

RICE – Stock up on the rice. It makes for a plentiful meal and will keep you going. Also, make note of the fact that white rice has a longer shelf life than brown.

HONEY – This should be a must for your stock. Honey is a natural probiotic, anti-bacterial, and anti-fungal. Also, it has healing properties when placed on external wounds. And best of all, it lasts forever!

FLOUR – Flour has a long shelf life and can be used to make many things. You should have some on hand!

POWDERED MILK – Milk is great for calcium and other nutrients, but it expires fast and needs to stay cold. However, powered milk is always ready to go with just some added water!

CANNED GOODS – It goes without saying that canned foods should be in your supplies. Most canned food has expiration dates of a few years, and most are best by, rather than use by. If it's best by, then all you have to worry about is a decrease in flavor. Also, NEVER eat from a bulged can. A common and notorious bacteria known to get inside cans will produce a toxin that is deadly. So check your cans and look for and feel for bulges. If bulged, throw away!

PASTA – You can't go wrong with noodles! They have a long shelf life along with many different variations, and will keep some fat on you. Stock up on Ramen and Mac-N-Cheese for flavor.

FLAVOR ENHANCERS – This is not a necessity for your supply in any way, shape, or form. This is simply a comfort factor item. I wanted to add this more for the sake of if there are children in your party like mine. Water is bland, and anything to make your parties children a little happier in such a world, is welcomed.

PEANUT BUTTER – You can never go wrong with peanut butter! Unless, of course, you're allergic, then stay away from it. But aside from that, peanut butter is a huge source of protein, has a long shelf life, and the taste is amazing!

OATS – Another great food source with a long shelf life.

OLIVE OIL – You might want some of this handy for any cooking. Little things go a long way.

IODIZED SALT – This is great for helping preserve and also simply as a flavor enhancer for bland food, like plain noodles for example. Also on the plus side, it lasts forever.

CORNMEAL – This should be stored right along with your flour, and it also has a longer shelf life than flour as well.

PET FOOD – Yes, pet food. You may have pets in your group that will be with you or that you'll take to your safe house. Also, most won't consider this option when local supplies run thin. When it comes to it, raid a pet store! It might not necessarily be the best in taste, but it has everything in it that you need to survive.

You should at the very least stock up enough that your group can stay holed up at the safe house for at least a few months. No one wants to go out raiding for food while the chaos is still at its highest points. Within a month or two, if not sooner depending on the speed of infection, there would be total collapse of government and law. At this time, the chaos will begin to lower in the sense of panicked crowds and martial law. Now, with that threat gone, it's a little safer to raid the landscapes of deserted buildings to see what's left.

Make sure you also ration your supply equally and safely within the group. Carefully calculate how to make what you have safely last a few months, or close to it. The last things you will want to do is burn through the supply and have to go out looking for more, among chaotic martial law, bandits, and zombies.

SECTION SIX

SURVIVAL GEAR

Weapons, ammunition, and food are not the only thing you should have in your stock pile. There are many items you are going to want to make sure you have when everything goes from bad to worse. In this section, like previous ones, we will compile a list of things you should consider having in your gear.

<u>COMPASS</u> – A few of these would be highly recommended. If your safe house perimeters are breached and your group gets temporarily split up, it would be nice to know what direction you are going, and what direction your back up safe house idea is in.

<u>FLASHLIGHTS</u> – This is another that should go without saying; one of these could save your life when the lights eventually go out. Even in daylight hours, you will need flashlights to raid buildings for food and supply. Use small ones to attach to your firearms.

<u>BATTERIES</u> – Those above mentioned flashlights won't do your group much good without batteries. Make sure you at least have a small box with all different types.

MESS KIT – Canned goods are fine to eat cold if it comes to that, but with a couple pots and pans, you can at least cook things up; especially game you've killed, which is a must to cook.

FISHNG LINE & HOOKS – Even if you don't have a rod, at least stock away some line and hooks. You can create a makeshift rod from practically anything, but without line and hooks, you better get that old spear out.

BLANKETS/PILLOWS – Gather some blankets and pillows in a large box for your supply, warmth and comfort will play roles in survival; specifically the warmth. Go to the sporting goods section and stock some emergency thermal blankets, they are cheap and will reflect your body heat back to you.

ASPIRIN – Bottles of aspirin and the like are a must have! Injuries likely will occur, not to mention just the old fashioned headache and sinus allergies.

MEDICAL TAPE/GAUZE – Again, injuries and cuts will occur, and you don't need to be running around with an open wound while zombie blood is spraying.

FIRST-AID KITS – Minus the extra supply of tape and gauze, a few first-aid kits would be useful to just grab when the minor, or not so minor, injuries occur.

ANTI-SEPTIC SPRAY – You can't be too careful with an injury, don't get lazy with stocking medical supplies; it could save your life.

HYDROGEN PEROXIDE/RUBBING ALCOHOL – Keeping wounds clean of bacteria could mean life or death in a time like this. You can't afford an infection when people are counting on you.

PERSONAL HYGIENE – Although not a must, it would be nice to stay fresh for at least a little while. Deodorant is more for the fresh factor, but it's important to stay clean, so stock some bar soap, hand soap, and sanitizer for stop the spread of any germs.

TOOTHBRUSHES/TOOTH PASTE/FLOSS – Dental hygiene will be very important! If you have a dentist in your group that is fantastic for you, but most will not. Brush, floss, and rinse thoroughly! Just imagine trying to defend against zombies or bandits with an abscess tooth! This can also lead to serious complications!

LIGHTERS/MATCHES – You will need to start fires, and have light, so keep lighters and matches stocked. You'll be glad you did!

LANTERNS/CANDLES – As stated before, eventually the power grid will go down and the lights will go off. These will be your only light sources now, and remember to keep your light away from any openings to the outside. Don't risk attracting the dead or alerting bandits to your whereabouts.

LIGHT STICKS – This wonderful item could be a major help to you and your group, so grab them up! Once you crack them, they will last several hours and keep an area partially lit. These are also good when raiding a dark building, to illuminate hallways and rooms and still have free hands for your weapons.

CHAIN/LOCK – You may have to break the fence of your safe house when it comes time to obtain it, so keep some lengths of chains and locks to secure the fence or any breach in your fence. They can also be used to seal off double doors, and many other things.

ROPE/CORD – This is something to be used in the same department of the chains, but can have a million uses, one being to make snares to catch food.

SUPER GLUE- The only use this would have for you, is to quickly field dress a wound and seal it shut. Just for that alone, it's worth throwing in your supply stock.

WIRE CUTTER – This would be used to get into any fenced area you need access to quietly. Maybe even your own scouted safe house location.

FIRE STARTING KIT – These come with flint and/or magnesium. Sometimes you need a fire fast, but don't rely on it always, learn how to start a fire the old fashioned way!

WATER PURIFICATION TABLETS – If you're on the move, need water, and cannot boil it, this is your best bet! These could greatly benefit your group in many situations.

 CAN OPENER – Many cans today have tabs, but many more still do not. So, do yourself a favor and make opening those cans a lot easier. There are better things to do with your combat knife.

 DUCT TAPE – The possibilities of the use for duct tape are nearly endless, and who knows what role it could play for the survival of your group. Just put it in the stock pile!

 RAIN PONCHO – There will, naturally, be rainy days and nights. You will always have to have people on guard and patrol duty at all times. And although it's not recommended doing raids in the rain, especially at night, you never know when a situation may demand it.

 WORK GLOVES – Sometimes there will be messy work, like disposal of zombie bodies. When moving the zombie bodies to a pile to burn, you will surely want some thick gloves!

 TWO-WAY RADIOS – This luxury won't last forever, but use it while you can. Two-way radios will greatly improve safety on raids and around the safe house.

 MRE's – Meals Ready to Eat are considered great things to stock up on. They usually come in bulk and are not always cheap; the plus side, however, is their long shelf life.

BACKPACK – Storing some backpacks with important supplies like first-aid kit, water, and other essentials, is a wise idea. One reason for this is the possible need to bug out and take what you can at a moment's notice, due to being breached and overrun by a horde, or pushed out by bandits. The next reason is because your scavenge teams will eventually have to start to travel further out to find food and supplies, so they should have a few of these in case they get pinned down somewhere and can't make it back for a day or two. And if they can't get out of the jam, this will hold them over until another group is formed to go and assist them.

SEEDS – packets of vegetable and fruit seeds will be something you need to start growing your own food. This is one of the most important things you should have in your survival stock.

GASOLINE – When the time comes to bug out and go, your vehicle might be running low, so keep some full gas cans around just in case. Better safe than sorry!

FLARE GUN – You never know when something like this could be useful, especially when in a cornered situation. A flare would likely distract a horde and maybe lead them away from an area in which you need access. Perhaps one of your scavenge teams get caught in a pinch and the radios no longer work, now they can signal…but be careful with this tactic, zombies will see the flare as well.

SPRAY PAINT – This isn't important, but can still be useful to mark locations you've fully cleared out.

PORTABLE RADIO/CB RADIO – One of these will help you keep track of the chaos outside and when things start to calm down, so you should consider one or both of these.

GEIGER COUNTER – No, zombie are not radioactive. However, when the system collapses and everything goes dark, there will be no one to man the nuclear power plants. Now the reactors will go down and there will be serious problems. You'll want to know when you're in such an area. Lastly, before the world governments collapse, in a desperate attempt to try and turn the tide, some nations may resort to nuclear attacks on high zombie population areas.

Maybe you should add a few gas masks, just in case! **BE PREPARED!**

SECTION SEVEN

PROTECTIVE WEAR

Now that you have what you need to defend your group, food, and survival gear, we need to go over protective wear! I hardly think you would want to roam into dark corridors to scavenge, never knowing where a zombie may be lurking, without protecting yourself to the fullest of your ability. You need to be thinking about more than just being bitten, as we'll go over in this section.

SAFETY GLASSES – Don't take the risk of zombie blood spraying in your eyes, which in effect, will likely infect you. Play it smart!

DUST MASK – You can breathe fine with these, and now you'll eliminate the risk of infected blood getting on or in your mouth.

FACE SHIELD – This will kill two birds with one stone, if you want to purchase some of these. They are a little more expensive, of course, but well worth the investment.

PAINTBALL MASK – This is one of the best ways to go for protecting your face. They are typically cheaper than a face shield, easy to breathe and protects your eyes and mouth. After all, they are already designed to protect from splatter effect in the mouth region.

 FOREARM GUARDS – If you're going to be reaching into dark places, or if you're prone to letting your guard down, then invest in these. They will be effective in protecting you from a bite.

 ELBOW/KNEE PADS – Don't risk tripping and falling on a raid and cracking a knee or elbow. A knee wound is serious and will drastically slow you down, allowing ghouls to catch up to you.

 SHIN GUARDS – People tend to hit their shins on a regular basis, and this is before the apocalypse. Also, these could protect your shins in low light conditions where you may not notice a crawling ghoul.

 LEATHER JACKET – These will also be very helpful in protecting you from bites, so if you have one, great! If not, you should invest. Lastly, they will keep you very warm in the winter.

 GAS MASK – As stated in the previous section, nuclear fallout of some magnitude will happen. Have some on board just in case.

 CHEMICAL SUIT – You can find disposable suits for a low cost, and you'll be glad you took the time to order some when you need to move zombie bodies and clean blood from an area.

Just think practical when it comes to protecting your body when you're away from the safe house. Don't act macho and brave just to try and prove some point, that kind of thinking will easily get you killed. Use your head, think before you act, and assess every location carefully before you raid it. People are depending on you, never forget that when you're feeling impatient.

SECTION EIGHT

BUILD YOUR GROUP

When there is confusion, chaos, and little order among your group, this can and will lead to serious problems. Your group needs to know all risks, roles, rules, and responsibilities. The best thing to do is make your group a democracy. The system has fallen, and you and your group are now on your own and must take care of each other.

Some groups may prefer to have one specific person namely in charge, or perhaps a few, to make some tough calls, but the entire group should all have a vote in anything that's decided. In a post-apocalyptic world, most choices will be hard ones, sit down and decide together. It's up to you whether or not the votes are unanimous or majority rules, but put a system together and work as a whole.

In this section we will go over roles for your group, based on skills and knowledge.

LEADERS – Leaders should be person/persons that work well with each other and the group, are dedicated to protecting the group by any means, and able to make the toughest choices when the vote is complete.

MEDICAL TEAM – Anyone in your group who has medical training or knowledge should naturally be in the medical team and mostly stay at the safe house. If you have many people with medical training, one should at least accompany scavenge teams.

SNIPERS – Your best marksmen should always be on duty and rotating shifts at high points around your safe house. This added security will keep your group and shelter much safer.

SCAVENGE PARTIES – Your group will need one or more teams, depending on the size of your group, to go out raiding buildings and homes for supplies. This would include people knowing how to use various weapons, to defend themselves and the team, and what to look for when it comes to supplies.

RATION COUNTER – Take one or two of the group who are the best at math to carefully ration the supplies among the group.

CHILD CARE – if there are a few or more children in your group, parents will be, naturally, looking out for their children, but assign anyone who's good with children and stays at the shelter to always be around them. Remember, however, children should be monitored and watched out for by the whole of the group as well.

COOKS – For those that enjoy cooking and/or are good at it, rotate cooking nights...everyone needs roles and duties.

PATROL – Having a patrol team will also add to the enduring security of your safe house. Members of the scavenge teams can work in shifts, day and night, to walk the perimeter of the shelter and make sure everything is secure.

GARDENERS – All the green thumbs among your group can tend to a garden for added food to your stock.

INVENTORY – Assign someone to take inventory and make sure rations are going out properly.

FABRICATION – If your group has some carpenters and/or welders, they can become a fabrication team, making your safe house all the safer. You can't go wrong with reinforced walls and fences.

STRATEGISTS – Whoever is well suited for coming up with strategies should work together in a team effort to map out routes and plan raids for the best efficiency.

Make sure teams are well thought out and be creative with forming other teams for certain tasks. Also, don't allow your group to be weak in any way by keeping people in their respective fields! The more knowledge your group has the safer they will be, so cross train everyone in the group.

For example, train the medical crew how to use weapons, ask the medical team to teach the scavenge teams how to use basic first-aid and how to field dress a wound. If someone doesn't know how to cook, teach them. Let the gardeners show others how to tend to crops, etc., etc., etc.

When everyone can do any ones role, your group is now a thousand times better off than it was were before!

SECTION NINE

CONDUCTING RAIDS

When it comes to raiding for supplies risks will always be a factor. The only thing you can do is be as cautious as possible, wear your protective gear, and don't take unnecessary actions that could get you killed. In this section we will cover some basic rules/regulations you should consider as a group for raids, as well as good places to raid, followed by places to avoid until you have little or no choice.

THINGS TO CONSIDER AS RAID REGULATIONS:

- NEVER RAID ALONE

- WORK AS A TEAM

- ONLY SPLIT UP IN TEAMS

- KEEP TWO PEOPLE OUTSIDE OF LOCATION ON WATCH

- DON'T USE FIREARMS UNLESS THERE IS NO OTHER CHOICE

- BE QUIET

- CLEAR THE LOCATION OF THREATS BEFORE LOOKING FOR GOODS

- WORK ONE AREA OR LEVEL AT A TIME

- KNOW WHERE ALL YOUR TEAM MATES ARE

- DON'T RUSH IT

These are simple basics, but add to them based on your groups' situation, location, and environment.

WHERE TO RAID

ISOLATED HOMES – If your group comes upon homes that are off to themselves and not in a large, possibly horde filled, residential area, these are good options. A lot of people will have fled from their home in search of rescue stations or evacuation points. If the house doesn't look fortified, it's likely empty. Don't assume that is it, however. Take proper precautions by calling out and seeing if someone may be inside, if so, leave them be. Homes that have been fled are great places to locate medicine, canned good, and other foods.

CONVENIENCE STORES – Small stores are scattered everywhere. Provided they weren't looted in the early parts of the disaster, you can find food, meds, and other useful things here. These are also a lot less likely to be inhabited by other survivors or bandits.

PHARMACIES- Most pharmacies are small, with the only downside being many are located in higher populace areas. You can, however, find them in small towns and on the outskirts of towns. They all carry important medicine your group will need and many also have food products to scavenge through. Pharmacies should be at the top of your list for raids before others loot them out. Medicine will always be needed and you may have members of your group that depend on certain medications like insulin.

 CAMP GROUNDS/PARK OFFICES – These building are scattered all throughout state parks and are likely places to find first-aid and other supplies. Parks are isolated and remote, so you shouldn't have a hard time with ghouls wandering around...though always be on the lookout for a wandering horde.

 POLICE STATIONS – If you can locate police stations that are in small rural areas or town outskirts, you should definitely plan a raid on it. Ammunition will begin to grow scarce and this is a good place to look for some, along with more guns and other weapons. While you're there, make sure you grab SWAT and riot gear for protective wear. An abandoned police station could help your group immensely!

 FIRE DEPARTMENTS – Firefighters are always on call and have shifts where they sleep at the department, so you could find food here. You will also be able to scavenge medical supplies here and from the ambulances. Take some fire axes, too!

 DINERS/RESTAURANTS – Remember that almost any former place of business had first-aid kits around, so always take a look for those. When it comes to small ma and pa diners and restaurants, you'll be able to scavenge canned goods, flour, salt, and other items.

HARDWARE STORES – If you see a hardware store, your group should be eager to plan a visit. You can find a lot of useful products here to ensure the safety of your group. Crowbars, axes, hatchets, machetes, and so many other tools and weapons you can scavenge. Add to the list things like lumber, metal material, fencing, and barbed wire to help with fortification and fabricating.

PET STORES – As stated earlier, when food supplies run low, pet food has all the protein and nutrients you need…even if it doesn't taste so great. Also, your group may have family pets that were brought along.

SPORTING GOODS STORES – These are another option to find ammunition and firearms if you cannot raid any police stations. As a bonus, you can restock arrows and crossbow bolts here, along with emergency equipment like flares, thermal blankets, first-aid, among many other things.

You will be able to find many places to raid for supplies that are moderately safer than others, look for abandoned homes on back roads and outside of towns first and foremost for the least risks. Don't forget to use spray paint to mark the places you have already raided, as not to waste your time later on. If you live in the country, or near country, you are fortunate as you will find many abandoned houses to raid along all the back roads and even main roads between towns.

WHERE TO AVOID…

AS LONG AS POSSIBLE

Here we are going to go over a list of high risk places. Eventually, you may not have a choice but to raid these locations but I advise doing so only under that circumstance. Unless all other options and resources have been depleted or a situation demands it, I wouldn't take the risk.

 HOSPITAL – Hospitals are, generally, huge. Many would have become trapped here when the plague began, while others would have flocked here with mounting injuries sustained in the ensuing chaos. If you don't know where you're going a hospital is nothing more than a maze…with plenty of dead ends to get yourself cornered. As with any location you raid you should consider the layout and weigh the risks. Sure, a hospital will have enough medical supply for an army but you have no clue how many walking corpses are roaming the halls or creeping in the hundreds of rooms. If you have no other choice but to raid a hospital, take a lot of extra time to plan the raid carefully! Make sure you have depleted other locations first, like small med centers and doctors' offices. If you can avoid raiding a hospital, do it!

 SCHOOLS – Overall, schools would be a considerable waste of time. The only likely thing inside that could benefit your group would be first-aid kits and some medical supply. If you have no other options, then raid it…a school isn't a place that should be overrun with ghouls but there could still be some inside or around, and schools are rather large.

 APARTMENT BUILDINGS – The average apartment building is in populated areas or very close to them. Many would have likely rushed these buildings in search of loved ones, which may have resulted in mass panic, injuries, and attacks by ghouls. These darkened hallways and apartments could hold many wandering zombies and are best to just avoid altogether.

MALLS/SHOPPING CENTERS – Again, being generally located in the midst of higher population zones, they are a huge risk. The shopping centers are a good place for food and medical supplies, but the layout is large and many lurking ghouls could be wandering the aisles. As for malls, there is absolutely no logical reason to go here. Avoid the mall.

TRAILER PARK – It wouldn't take much to get surrounded inside a trailer park, and they could be easily infested with the living dead. These you need to be weary of and tread carefully and quietly. Although not as risky as a hospital or apartment complex, they are not to be taken upon lightly by any means.

HOUSING DEVELOPMENTS – The same basic issues apply here that go with trailer parks, other than the fact the homes are larger and a bit more spaced out. Hordes of dead are likely roaming the areas; so again, stay as quiet as possible and out of sight.

MILITARY BASES – If you are completely sure one of these are abandoned, it is worth checking out for the potential to scavenge ammunition, weapons, and medical supply. Working in your favor is a fence that has kept zombie out, but that doesn't mean there aren't any inside! The main reason to avoid military bases would be the uncertainty of whether or not it's occupied by surviving soldiers, or other survivors, who may deem you a contagion threat and shoot first, ask later. On a final note, if it's a small base, and abandoned, it could make for a great safe house if the conditions are right!

 OFFICE BUILDINGS – Large, multi-storied, and dead ends...with the most in reward being first-aid kits, which are not worth the risk to raid. If the building is in the city, people will likely have become trapped here like in other locations. Office buildings are best left alone.

 NURSING HOMES – This presents the same problem as a hospital and is bound to have zombies inside. Small nursing homes are doable with lower risk, but the larger they are the more danger you're putting yourselves in. Unless necessary, steer clear.

 LARGE TOWNS – As time goes by, most of the dead will begin to migrate out of towns in search for food, but it doesn't mean towns will be empty. Keep large towns toward the bottom of your list for raids, and then scavenge them house by house over time for supplies.

 CITIES – Hopefully your group is never forced to having to scavenge inside a large city. Cities have high populations, of course, and will be filled with ghouls. As with towns, some of the dead will migrate out, wandering aimlessly, for food. But the city will still be occupied by enough of them to quickly overrun your group, not to mention bandits that will have safe houses set up within the city could pose serious problems for you as well.

No place you raid will be without risk. No place is completely safe.

However, some are safer than others and you'll have to use your best judgment when considering all your options. Be prepared, plan ahead, stay vigilant, and keep a cool head. The better prepared and planned you are the safer your raids will be!

SECTION TEN

ZOMBIE CAUSES

In the not so distant past, it was thought that a zombie apocalypse could never happen...but with advances in science many scientists today say it may not be plausible, but it *is* possible! So this brings the question, debated by experts, what could cause a zombie apocalypse? Let's take a look!

<u>VIRUS</u> – Viruses are considered high on the list for causing such an event... and with good reason! Consider the furious rabies virus with symptoms that include fever, irritability, and violence! Now imagine that same rabies virus has mutated and acts far more quickly within its host and you have a formula for a zombie pandemic. Another factor to make viruses more of a threat is how quickly they can mutate and evolve; making them hard to fight with medicine once they gain a resistance.

<u>PARASITE</u> – These are nasty little creatures that could easily take control of a host to use it for its own gain. Consider the parasite known as *Toxoplasmosa Gondii*. This parasite is only able to breed within the digestive tract of cats. So how does it get there? They infect rats and

then completely take over the brains of the rats and guide them on a search for cats, so as to be devoured. This is a real parasite that exists today...imagine the possibilities of what a new breed of parasite could do to cause a pandemic.

NEUROGENESIS – Labs around the world have been experimenting with stem cell research and research into reanimation, but the continuous problem? The brain dies from the outside in, killing the human parts and leaving basic primitive instinct.

FUNGUS – There is a fungus known as *Ophiocordyceps Unilateralis* that infects ants. The fungal cells attack and take over the brain and then force the ant to bite into a leaf and stay that way until it dies. This infects the leaf, waiting for another ant to eat and then infect. Imagine, if you will, a new or evolved species of fungi that releases seemingly harmless spores into the air. Okay, now for this hypothetical theory, thousands of these spores are inhaled but perhaps they go dormant. Now, what if these dormant spores were to activate upon the hosts death and begin their work? Now we have a very scary scenario. With other body functions stopped, the growing network of the fungus could begin to carry nutrients where needed. Soon, the network would reach the brain where it could activate the primitive parts. It would be driven to feed, and the said network could extract nutrients from meat to help slow down decomposition. These spores could also be spread through bite and blood.

NANOTECHNOLOGY – These microscopic machines are being designed to go inside humans and repair damage, which does sound like an amazing thing...but what if it went completely wrong? These are machines that can self-replicate and have artificial intelligence. Some experiments have shown them still active and functioning for over a month after a host dies, and they are capable of building...and destroying. It's been said that in under a decade they could have nanobots enter a brain and build neural pathways and connections. If these bots can function after death, and become a dangerous threat, they could create pathways to control the body. Being that nanobots self-replicate, they can in turn spread themselves via bites. Nanobots could help the betterment of the world...or end it.

Many things could cause a zombie apocalypse, so nothing should be ruled out. It would be easy to assume that such a virus, fungus, or parasite developing and evolving in nature, has a rare chance...but what about nanotechnology and neurogenesis research? Scientists are always working on possible bio-weapons or experimenting with cross breeding viruses. The zombie virus, or fungus, doesn't have to happen in nature when we have scientists that could intentionally or accidently make one. And then what happens when it escapes? Or is released? We have an apocalypse! Look at all the damage mankind has done, the dangerous things we've created...why would it surprise anyone if we caused such an outbreak?

SECTION ELEVEN

SURVIVOR COMMUNITY

Once things have settled more over time you will want to consider better living arrangements. This is especially true if your group was already large, or perhaps you've picked up other survivors that have added to your numbers. In any case, you'll want better suited living conditions than a prison, storage unit, or one single fortified farm house can provide.

In order to build a fortified small community you will need to be in the countryside and it will take a lot of time and work to accomplish, but it will all be worth it once it's complete. When it comes to building a survivor community you really have two great options to choose from to best fit your group. Neither option will be easy, nor built over night.

That being said, option one is clearing out a small town; and I do mean small! Remember, too big is too risky, just like a safe house. You have to make your community as safe and defendable as you possibly can. A small housing development, outside of a major city, would suffice. Option two would be country property lined on one side with multiple homes or duplexes. Another great choice would be a cul-de-sac with multiple houses lined around it.

After choosing which option you wish to take, or have available, the work begins. Firstly, you will naturally have to clear the area of all ghouls. Don't rush it, take your time...clearing it out will likely be the most dangerous part. After it is clear, you need to dispose of all the bodies, and do it far away from your soon to be community. Next is fortification. Your community will need protected by walls all the way around. The fabricators of your group will know how to put up rows of reinforced fencing. Another option is obtaining shipping containers, or easier to transport, semi-trailers, to turn on their sides as walls. These will be far more defendable than fencing.

Also, with shipping containers, you can post guards on them from the north, east, south, and west at all times. You'll also need a front gate, which will be the weakest point of your complex, for entering and leaving. This gate should be manned at all times, and held shut with chains and padlocks.

Once you have everything ready to be defended and guarded you can start moving in from your safe house. Now your group will be a little more comfortable and feeling more secure. With multiple homes for people to live, yards for kids to play, and land to grow crops, not only will your group feel more secure and safe, but morale will go up as well.

Now, along with homes, you can set up guard posts inside by less secure areas if need be. If there are extra homes or buildings, they can be made into a hospital, recreation center, or day care if your group has multiple children. Maybe you would like to set up a type of work out building to stay in shape.

If you're lucky your new community will be around a water source that hasn't been contaminated, but it's wise to still collect rain water...a lake, pond, or stream could become a hazard at any given time. Most of these country areas have well water but, again, make sure it's not contaminated and always boil any water you find.

Your group will become all the more strong working as a community, and the bonds you've formed will also grow. Everyone will sleep a little bit better and feel a lot more rested. Having a community will be the best thing your group can achieve. It will put you in a better position to help other survivors, grow in numbers, and even expand your community over time. If all goes well, you'll have a permanent home to build upon!

However, this is not an invitation to let your guard down, or pretend that the world is back to normal. Don't forget the threats right outside your community. You're a little bit safer, a little bit more secure...but beyond your gates are hordes of flesh eaters, and bandits that may want your wonderful new set up!

SECTION TWELVE

AFTERMATH

The world as you knew it is over. Running water and electricity are now a rare luxury at best, while television and the like are dusty relics of the past. Nothing is going to go back to the way it once was...at least not for a very, very long time. Pockets of communities will be built but the dead will still be walking and hunting for food.

It will be important that we not lose our humanity as we strive to survive. In defense of our loved ones and ourselves, we may have been forced to do horrible things, but not unless we had no other option. In a world without order what choice would we have? Our humanity will keep us alive, help us survive, and help us guide our youths in whatever is left among the ruins of the world.

It will be important to teach any children in the group all the skills they will need to withstand against the harsh new landscapes. They will need weapons training, agricultural skills, and social skills, among many more. Just because the world has come to a halt doesn't mean that learning has. Teach reading and writing, they will still need it someday. Although most would be appalled by seeing their children carrying a firearm, it's a new world with new rules. If you want them to survive the living dead they'll need to know how to defend themselves and grow up faster than they should have to. Just as it was before the world came crashing down, they should still be taught not to speak with people they do not know. Even more so now! Teach them to trust their instincts, be kind, but cautious and vigilant!

In this post-apocalyptic world you will be living in, all bets are off. You can only do the best you can with what you have and hope and pray for the best. Write things down about what once was and how things were. Collect literature, including history books so the children can see how things once looked, how the system worked, and perhaps what led to this event.

The world you knew is gone...but you're not...so never quit, never give up, and don't stand down!

SECTION THIRTEEN

ANCIENT TEXTS

"And the Lord will send a plague on all the nations that fought against Jerusalem. Their people will become like walking corpses, their flesh rotting away. Their eyes will rot in their sockets, and their tongues will rot in their mouths. On that day they will be terrified, stricken by the Lord with great panic. They will fight their neighbors hand to hand." - Zechariah 14:12-13

"The earth will give birth to her dead. Go, my people, enter your rooms and shut the doors behind you; hide yourselves for a little while until his wrath has passed by." - Isaiah 26:20

"Your covenant with death will be annulled; your agreement with the grave will not stand. When the overwhelming scourge sweeps by, you will be beaten down by it. As often as it comes it will carry you away; morning after morning, by day and by night, it will sweep through." - Isaiah 28:18-19

"I will raise the dead and they will eat the living. And the dead will outnumber the living." – Epic of Gilgamesh. 2100 BC

"Appearing at the time of the great games of slaughter: Not far from the age of the great millennium, when the dead will come out of their graves." – Nostradamus

"On the Day the Summoner summons them to something unspeakably terrible, they will emerge from their graves with downcast eyes, like swarming locusts, necks outstretched, eyes transfixed, rushing headlong to the Summoner. The disbelievers will say, 'This is a pitiless day!'" – The Quran

SECTION FOURTEEN

RULES TO SURVIVE BY

Every group will have their own rules and regulations suited to their needs, situation, and surroundings. The rules of a group would differ, and be stricter, depending on where you're located. For example, rules for surviving in a city environment would surely have a longer and stricter list than for those in the country. Many rules though would be the same, and here are some basics to consider:

1. <u>NEVER GO ALONE</u> – Trying to raid a location or wandering too far on your own could lead to disaster. Not informing someone of your whereabouts and then ending up surrounded by a horde, or attacked by bandits, could spell your demise. Always use the buddy system!

2. <u>WATCH YOUR INVENTORY</u> – Take care to always check your food and medical supply, and carefully ration equally as needed.

3. <u>SHARPEN YOUR BLADES</u> – Blades naturally get dull after long periods of use, especially when cutting through bone, so sharpen regularly.

4. <u>CLEAN GUNS</u> – your firearms can save your life...be it zombie and bandit defense, or finding food to eat. Always take good

care of your weapons!

5. **<u>DON'T TAKE EXTREME RISKS</u>** – Taking risks will now be a part of life, but when you don't need to take one, don't! If you need to get from one point to another, with a ghoul in between, leave the lone ghoul be and go around it.

6. **<u>KEEP YOUR GUARD UP</u>** – it would be easy to feel completely safe with a well-fortified safe house or community, but that kind of thinking could get you killed. It's fine to relax in your new confines and take a load off, but never let your guard completely down. As stated earlier, your location will never be completely safe and impenetrable. A large enough horde, or big enough group of bandits, could overtake your defenses!

7. **<u>MAINTAIN CHILD SUPERVISION</u>** – If children are a part of your group, they should be under the care of others and watched at all times. Young children will naturally underestimate the dangers of this new world and get bored and wander. Don't let them out of your sight!

8. **<u>KNOW WHO TO TRUST</u>** – New survivors may over time be introduced in your group, and sometimes you may happen upon ones that are trouble. Trust your instincts on new comers and keep your eye on them. Eventually they will either prove themselves good for the group or a danger.

9. **<u>STAY SOBER</u>** – Don't put your life and others at risk with substance abuse. If you have a responsibility such as guarding, patrol, or raiding, all the while intoxicated, you're nothing more than a danger to the group.

10. **<u>DON'T PANIC</u>** – One of the most important rules is to keep your head. Stay calm, think fast, and never panic!

Again, these are basic rules you might find in any group, but you'll surely have many more in order to ensure group safety. Sometimes people don't like rules, but certain ones will keep you alive. If a new comer doesn't like the rules you have in place you can always tell him he's more than welcome to take his chances outside and hope to find another group somewhere. Don't make exceptions for people, especially new comers you don't even know. It's your safe house or survivor community and your responsibility to keep your people safe.

SECTION FIFTEEN

YOUR CHECKLIST

For those looking to start preparing here is a complimentary checklist for you to us:

FOOD

- ☐ **Bottled Water**
- ☐ **Dried Beans**
- ☐ **Rice**
- ☐ **Honey**
- ☐ **Flour**
- ☐ **Powdered Milk**
- ☐ **Canned Foods**
- ☐ **Pasta**
- ☐ **Flavor Enhancers**
- ☐ **Peanut Butter**
- ☐ **Oats**
- ☐ **Olive Oil**

- ☐ Iodized Salt
- ☐ Cornmeal
- ☐ Pet Food
- ☐ Sugar
- ☐ Wheat
- ☐ Dry Corn
- ☐ Baking Soda

WEAPONS

- ☐ Crowbar
- Machete
- Combat Knife
- Shotgun
- Rifle
- Pistol
- Revolver
- Crossbow
- Bow and Arrow
- Katana
- High Powered Air Rifle

- Hammer
- Axe
- Hatchet
- ☐ Slingshot

GEAR/MEDICAL

- Compass
- Flashlights
- Batteries
- Mess kit
- ☐ Fishing Line
- ☐ Fishing Hooks
- ☐ Blankets
- ☐ Thermal Blankets
- ☐ Pillows
- ☐ Aspirin
- ☐ Antibiotics
- ☐ Medical Tape
- ☐ Gauze
- ☐ First-Aid Kits

- ☐ Antiseptic Spray
- ☐ Hydrogen Peroxide
- ☐ Rubbing Alcohol
- ☐ Bar Soap
- ☐ Hand Soap
- ☐ Hand Sanitizer
- ☐ Tooth Brushes
- ☐ Tooth Paste
- ☐ Floss
- ☐ Vitamins
- ☐ Bandages
- ☐ Toilet Paper
- ☐ Lighters
- ☐ Matches
- ☐ Lanterns
- ☐ Candles
- ☐ Light Sticks
- ☐ Chains
- ☐ Locks
- ☐ Rope
- ☐ Cord

- ☐ Super Glue

- ☐ Wire Cutter

- ☐ Fire Starting Kit

- ☐ Water Purification Tablets

- ☐ Can Opener

- ☐ Duct Tape

- ☐ Rain Poncho

- ☐ Work Gloves

- ☐ Two-Way Radios

- ☐ MRE's

- ☐ Backpack

- ☐ Seeds

- ☐ Gasoline

- ☐ Flare Gun

- ☐ Flares

- ☐ Spray Paint

- ☐ Portable Radio

- ☐ CB Radio

- ☐ Cards/Games (for down time)

- ☐ Geiger Counter

PROTECTIVE WEAR

- ☐ Safety Glasses
- ☐ Dust Masks
- ☐ Face Shield
- ☐ Paintball Mask
- ☐ Forearm Guards
- ☐ Elbow Pads
- ☐ Knee Pads
- ☐ Shin Guards
- ☐ Leather Jacket
- ☐ Gas Mask
- ☐ Chemical Suit

CLOSING

There's an old saying...never say never! What science experts once said was impossible has been bumped up to possible but improbable. The day may come when they announce the improbable has occurred...and is spreading quickly! In closing, we live in troubled and scary times with threats of nuclear war, super storms, and economic collapse. New diseases are discovered all the time and could show themselves at any given moment. The information presented within these pages will not only help you survive a plague of the living dead, undead or alive, but will also serve to help you in any disaster or apocalyptic event. Be it nuclear world war, a volcanic winter from the Yellowstone super volcano erupting, or perhaps a meteor strike.

Simply put...if you're prepared for the Zombie Apocalypse...you're prepared for anything!